Contents

KU-377-842

Introducing Skateboarding

Imagine you're a Californian surfer. You like nothing better than to paddle out to the break and catch a wave. But what do you do when the ocean is as flat as a pancake? Wouldn't it be great if you could turn roadways into roadwaves for nonstop surf action?

That's exactly how the sport of skateboarding got its start. During the 1950s, restless surfers stuck wooden boxes on to rollerskate wheels. They rode their 'skateboards' after the day's surfing was done. The new sport took off. By 1963, you could buy fancy skateboards across North America. The boards even came in customised designs for different riding styles, such as downhill or freestyle.

Skateboarding did not always enjoy such a smooth ride, though. The sport almost died several times. But it was reborn, again and again, each time in more exhilarating ways.

Skaters can do the most amazing acrobatic tricks on the vert ramp.

NEW WORDS

Grind: To ride on a ledge or rail in such a way that only the trucks touch, making a grinding noise.

Skateboarding

Helaine Becker

W
FRANKLIN WATTS
LONDON • SYDNEY

This edition first published in 2013
by Franklin Watts

Copyright © 2013
Brown Bear Books Ltd

Franklin Watts
338 Euston Road
London NW1 3BH

Franklin Watts Australia
Level 17/207 Kent Street
Sydney, NSW 2000

A CIP catalogue record for this book is available
from the British Library.

Dewey no: 796.22

ISBN 978 1 4451 2354 7

Printed in China

Franklin Watts is a division of Hachette Children's Books,
an Hachette UK company.
www.hachette.co.uk

Note to parents and teachers concerning websites:
In the book every effort has been made by the Publishers to
ensure that websites are suitable for children, that they are
of the highest educational value, and that they contain no
inappropriate or offensive material. However, because of the
nature of the Internet, it is impossible to guarantee that the
contents of these sites will not be altered. We advise that
Internet access is supervised by a responsible adult.

For Brown Bear Books Ltd:
Designer: Lynne Lennon
Picture Researcher: Sean Hannaway
Editor: Leon Gray
Managing Editor: Tim Cooke
Art Director: Jeni Child
Design Manager: David Poole
Children's Publisher: Anne O'Daly
Editorial Director: Lindsey Lowe

Every effort has been made to trace the owners
of copyrighted material.

Photo credits

Front cover: Branimir Kvartuc/PA Photos
Backgrounds: Christian Carroll/iStockphoto

Action Images: Lucy Nicholson 4–5, 8, 14–15, Mike Blake 7bl;
Action Plus: Neil Tingle 6; Alamy: S. Kuttig 16, Joe Tree 20–21,
David Young-Wolff 23t, Buzz Pictures 26; Buzz Pictures: Styley
12; ClimaxMfg: 9t; Corbis: Sam Diephuis 13t, 15, Roy Morsch
13b, John-Francis Bourke 17, Martin Philbey 18, Sergey
Dolzhenko 19, Duomo 23b; Gasoline Alley Antiques: 11b;
Getty Images: Tony Duffy 5, Bill Ray 7tr, Jeanne Rice 22,
Tina Schmidt 24, Donald Miralle 29b; Movie Store Collection:
Amblin 28; OC Ramps Inc: 25t, 25b; PA Photos: Gero Breloer
29t; Rex Features: David Thorpe 7cr, Pekka Sakki 10, Neale
Haynes 27; Shutterstock: Alexander Kalina 9b; Warren Bolster:
Concrete Wave Editions 11t

Illustrations: Mark Walker 11, 19

LOOK CLOSER

Olympic sport

Not all skaters like the idea of skateboarding being an Olympic sport. They think it might force their sport to fit into an approved 'mould'. Many would like to keep the sport the way it is — independent and freewheeling. But if skateboarding were an Olympic sport, it would receive a lot more funding. Many more skaters might be able to turn the sport they love into a career.

Skateboard industry

Today, skateboarding is a multimillion-pound industry. Top skaters are professionals who can make a career through prize money and sponsorship deals. Skateboarding might even become an Olympic sport. So get ready for a thrilling ride through the world of **half-pipes** and **half-cabs**, flips and turns, and slides and **grinds**.

Skateboarding has been a popular sport for many decades.

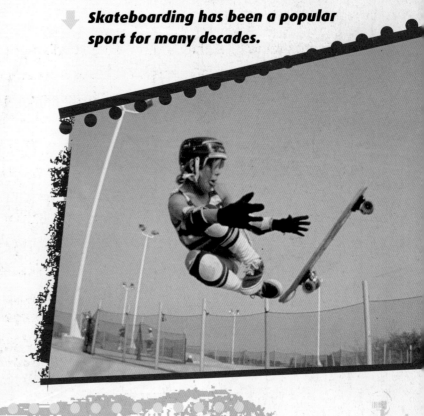

Half-cab: A ramp trick named for skater Steve Caballero.
Half-pipe: A U-shaped ramp used for skateboard tricks.

Standing Room Only

The first **decks** were made from wood. These soon gave way to plastics and other materials that made the boards easier to ride. Most skaters now prefer original decks made from the wood of the maple tree.

The invention of the **kicktail** in the 1970s was a major breakthrough in skateboard design. The kicktail helps skaters turn and flip the board with ease. Another big development was adding grip tape. Grip tape helps the feet 'stick' to the deck.

The kicktail was added to the skateboard's basic design to make flips and turns much easier.

LOOK CLOSER

Making the board

1) Thin layers of maple are cut to shape.
2) Glue is applied to each layer.
3) The layers are stacked on top of each other.
4) The stack is placed in a mould.
5) The stack is pressed together while the glue dries.
6) Holes are drilled in the finished board to complete the deck.

NEW WORDS

Deck: The flat part of the skateboard on which the skater stands.

A gritty deck surface is helpful for doing tricks. So is a slippery underside. In the 1980s, a company called Santa Cruz released Everslick boards. They were made with a plastic undercoat. The coating lets the board slide across any surface.

Different decks

Skaters choose different decks for different riding styles. Vert skaters do tricks on ramps and other vertical or curved surfaces. They prefer wider decks. Street skaters mostly do tricks on flat ground. They like narrower decks that give a good 'pop' – a lift off when the board is flexed. Longboards are mostly used for downhill racing or **cruising**. They measure up to 1.8 metres (6 ft) long and are shaped like surfboards.

▼ *Modern decks are made from environmentally friendly materials such as bamboo.*

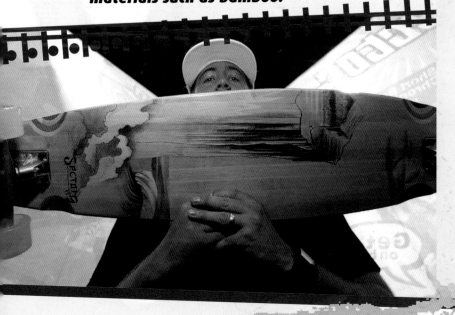

Stacking the decks

1950s–1960s	The earliest skateboards were made from shaped wood.
1970s	Brightly coloured banana boards made from flexible plastic became very popular. Ribs on the underside gave the deck support.
1970s	Most boards were made out of thin layers of maple that were glued together. Some included high-tech materials such as aluminium or fibreglass.
1980s	Decks became wider and longer for street skating. The upturned nose was added.
1990s–	Skateboard manufacturers produce decks in many different materials and shapes. Most have found that springy, strong maple is the best material for a smooth ride.

Kicktail: The rise at the back of the deck.
Cruising: Using your board to move from place to place.

Truck Technology

The trucks do much more than connect the wheels to the deck. Without trucks, the skateboard could not carve turns.

The trucks are the T-shaped metal housings that are found on the underside of the deck. The truck is made of three main parts: the baseplate, the hanger and the kingpin bolt.

The trucks bolt onto the underside of the deck.

Trucks apart

The baseplate is the flat part of the truck that bolts onto the deck. The hanger is attached to the baseplate. It holds the wheel **axles**. The hanger lies against a depression, called a pivot cup, in the baseplate. The pivot cup lets the hanger move in many directions. It works in a similar way to your shoulders, which let your arms

LOOK CLOSER

Chicago pivot

The basic truck design is based on the 'Chicago pivot'. This type of truck was invented for rollerskate ballroom dancing in the 1920s. Specially designed trucks for skateboards were not available in shops until 1975.

NEW WORDS

Axle: A rod that attaches to wheels and allows them to spin.
Bushing: A hollow sleeve used to reduce friction or motion in mechanical parts.

move in many directions. The last part of the truck is the kingpin bolt. It holds all the truck's parts together. Spongy pads around the kingpin, called **bushings**, cushion the pin when it moves. The softer the bushings, the easier it is to make the skateboard turn. The stiffer the bushings, the harder it is to carve that curve. You can change the bushings or adjust the kingpin nut for tighter turns or better control.

⬆ *These trucks are made from aluminium, which is soft and weak but good for grinding.*

LOOK CLOSER

Friction forces

When two objects rub against each other, there is always some **friction**. Friction slows things down and wastes energy. Bushings are important because they reduce friction between the skateboard's moving parts.

deck

baseplate

kingpin bolt

axle

hanger

Friction: The force that opposes the movement of two surfaces that are touching one another.

Wheels Revolution

The first skateboards had metal wheels, but they got rusty quickly and produced a bone-rattling ride. Next came clay wheels. They were much smoother, but they also wore out quickly. They were also dangerous, because they did not grip the road well.

In 1971, a California surfer named Frank Nasworthy remembered seeing **urethane** wheels being made at a plastics factory owned by his friend's father. He thought the urethane wheels would work better for skateboarding than metal or clay wheels. So Nasworthy put together his first boards with

Wheels come in a range of colours and styles.

LOOK CLOSER

How do bearings work?
Bearings reduce friction by putting smooth metal balls or rollers between two moving surfaces. The surfaces can then roll over the balls instead of sliding against each other.

NEW WORDS

Urethane: A hard-wearing plastic that can be moulded into different shapes.

Frank Nasworthy set up Cadillac Wheels in 1971.

urethane wheels. They were very fast but easy to control. Nasworthy invested about £500 – his earnings from a restaurant job – to start up Cadillac Wheels Company. By 1975, he was selling 300,000 sets of wheels a year.

Sealed wheels

Rough Rider bearings ushered in the next wheel revolution. Until 1975, the wheels used for skateboarding had ball

Clay wheels were common until urethane took over in the 1970s.

wheel nut · cone · wheel · cone · washer · ball bearings

Bearings make the ride much smoother.

bearings that dropped into the wheels. They were easily ruined by dirt from the road. Rough Rider's bearings were sealed inside the wheel. The innovation allowed the wheels to last longer and to go faster.

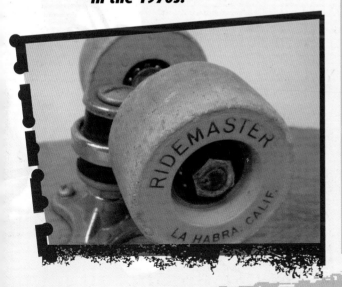

LOOK CLOSER

What is urethane?

Urethane is a kind of hard, rubbery plastic. It is very **resilient**. When a resilient material is compressed or stretched, it returns to its original shape quickly. Urethane wheels keep in contact with the road better than wheels made from other materials. They lose less energy so they spin faster. They also absorb shocks better, making for a smoother ride.

Resilient: Being able to return to an original shape or position.

Get a Grip

Most skateboarding shoes have vulcanized soles, which help to grip the deck.

Skateboarding savvy only starts with your skateboard. What you wear on your feet is also key to clever skating. Your shoes can make the difference between a perfect pop shove-it and a pride-popping face-plant.

Skateboarding shoes need three elements. They should keep your feet on the deck with stellar grip. They should cushion you from jarring **impact**. And the shoes have got to be durable to survive pounding during tough sessions.

Skate shoe makers

In 1966, shoe manufacturer Vans released the first shoes that were dedicated for skateboarding. Other companies, such as Airwalk and Vision, followed suit with their own designs in the 1980s. New designs and materials keep making skate shoes better and better every year.

NEW WORDS

Impact: When two objects hit each other, such as your feet and the ground.

LOOK CLOSER

Shoe spotting

Look for skate shoes with these features:
1) **Vulcanized** rubber soles stick to the board and resist wear.
2) Air or gel pockets and thick cushioning prevent heel bruising.
3) Lace loops and shoelace protectors stop laces from shredding.
4) Flexibility in the sole increases board 'feel'.

⬆ *Skate shoes are not just a fashion statement. They aid grip and protect the feet from hard knocks.*

⬇ *Some skaters prefer to ride barefoot.*

▶▶▶▶▶▶▶▶

FACT! Foot facts

· The first skaters rode barefoot to honour the sport's surfing roots.
· Sneakers are considered to be safety wear to prevent foot injuries.
· If you ride with your right foot forward you are called a 'goofy foot'.

Vulcanized: Soles with sulphur added to the rubber to make it harder, stronger and more stretchy.

Safe Skateboarding

Skateboarding is not all fun and games. Broken wrists and cracked heads are real risks for both new and advanced skaters alike. Safety wear is crucial for reducing the crunch factor.

Early skaters did not have skate-specific safety gear. The best they could do was borrow the gear from other sports. It did not always work. Riders got injured. Skate parks were shut down. The sport was even banned in some places. The problem was solved when skate-specific helmets and pads with plastic caps came on to the market.

LOOK CLOSER

Basic first aid for broken bones

After calling for help from an adult or 999, follow these procedures:
1) Stop the bleeding. Apply pressure to the wound with a clean cloth.
2) **Immobilise** the injured area.
3) Apply ice packs. Ice reduces pain and swelling.
4) Treat for shock. Make the person lie down. Position their head lower than their body. Raise their legs slightly if they are undamaged.

NEW WORDS

Immobilise: To prevent from moving.

Plastic protection

Knee pads and arm pads are made up of plastic caps that cover thick cushions. Since they reduce friction, the caps let you slide to safety if you fall. Wrist guards act like an **exoskeleton** to protect wrist joints. It is essential that new skaters wear the right gear. Even seasoned skaters should wear pads to protect against broken bones.

Helmet, armpads and kneepads – safety gear is vital to prevent injuries.

FACT!

Safety first

Unlike most other sports, there are no performance standards for skateboarding safety equipment. Choose your gear carefully!

LOOK CLOSER

Head protection

Helmets are designed to protect your head from hard knocks. An inner layer of foam absorbs energy and softens the blow to your brain. The best foam for board helmets is made from expanded polypropylene (EPP). A hard outer shell stands up to multiple impacts. A sturdy chin strap and buckle keep your helmet snugly in place. Keep it fastened at all times! A bright colour makes you easier to see while street skating. An ASTM F1492 sticker means the helmet is the safest.

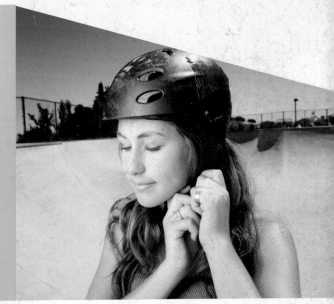

Exoskeleton: An outer skeleton or shell, like the shell of an insect.

Body Basics

Most skateboard professionals are serious athletes. They stay in shape and take care of their bodies to keep up with the demands of the sport. Take some tips from the top skaters before you tackle tricks of your own.

← *Skateboarding is tough on the body. Drinking water helps athletes stay hydrated.*

FACT!

►►►►►►►►►►

Nutrition facts

· **Dehydration** can reduce both the flexibility of your muscles and your **coordination**. Make sure to drink plenty of water!

· Junk food robs your body of the energy you would get from healthy food choices.

NEW WORDS

Dehydration: An unhealthy loss of water from the body.

Eat nutritious foods such as protein-rich meat, seafood and dairy items to fuel your body for long, hard sessions. Don't forget a variety of fruit and vegetables. Get energy from sources of carbohydrate, such as potatoes and oats. Enough sleep will help your body recover from wear and tear.

LOOK CLOSER

Stretching exercises

· *Ankle flex.* Sit on the floor with both legs fully extended. Lift one leg a few centimetres off the ground. Point your toe and use it to 'write' your name in the air. Repeat with other foot.

· *Back twist.* Sit on the floor with one leg out straight and the other crossed in front of you, with the sole of your foot on the floor. Use your opposite elbow to pull the knee into your body while you twist. Repeat on the other side.

· *Groin stretch.* Sit with the bottoms of your feet touching each other. Press down gently on your knees. Hold for 20 seconds.

· *Hamstring stretch.* Lie on your back. Raise one leg. Hold it for 20 seconds. Repeat with other leg.

· *Quad stretch.* Grasp one shin. Pull it back and up towards your rear until you feel a stretch in the front of your thigh. Hold for 20 seconds. Repeat with other leg.

Stretching warms the body up and helps to prevent injuries to the muscles.

Coordination: When the body and brain work together to balance and move.

Keeping Balance

Balance is key to great skateboarding. But you'll need to be one step ahead of your brain on a skateboard – it's hard to predict where there are bumps and dips on the ground. It's even harder keeping upright when you're trying out your next trick.

Foot stand

· Stand on one foot.
· Time yourself with a stopwatch.
· Imagine how much harder this test would be on a moving skateboard!

Your **centre of gravity** is the key to keeping balance. Its location varies based on your shape and **gender**, and it shifts whenever you move. The lower your centre of gravity, the easier it is to hold your balance. Crouch low to stay stable and improve your balance.

All in the ears

Inside your ear, semicircular canals are filled with fluid. When your head moves, so does the fluid. Its motion

Crouching down low helps to lower your centre of gravity.

NEW WORDS

Centre of gravity: The point in your body where your weight is centred.

18

stimulates hair cells in the walls of the canals. The cells send the information to your brain. Your brain then uses the information, along with other cues from your eyes, joints and muscles, to figure out your position in space.

Regular or goofy?

Lefties usually find it easier to balance when they ride goofy – with their right foot forward. Righties tend to prefer a regular stance – with their left foot forward.

LOOK CLOSER

Learning how to fall

When you lose your balance, protect yourself by learning how to take the fall.
1) Crouch down low so you won't have as far to fall.
2) Try to land on your shoulder and arm. Then roll to reduce the force of the impact.
3) Try not to brace your fall with your hands to avoid wrist injuries.
4) Stiffening up will cause greater damage to joints and muscles, so stay relaxed.

Regular   **Goofy**

⬆ *How do you ride — regular or goofy?*

⬇ **Your arms can help you stay balanced.**

▶▶▶▶▶▶▶▶▶

FACT!

Body balance

· Holding your arms like an airplane helps to maintain balance.
· Working out with a balance board can help you improve both your balance and coordination.

Gender: Whether someone is male or female.

On the Streets

A lot of street tricks seem to defy the laws of physics. In reality, skaters take advantage of physics to help them pull off the most amazing stunts.

When you pop an Ollie, you put a strong downwards force on the tail. In his laws of motion, **Sir Isaac Newton** states that 'for every action there is an equal and opposite reaction'. So when the tail pushes down against the ground, the ground pushes up against the

It takes time and practice to pop the perfect Ollie.

NEW WORDS

Sir Isaac Newton (1642-1727): English scientist who came up with the three laws of motion.

board with an equal and opposite force. When you jump, the upwards force is able to overcome the force of **gravity**. The board pops into the air.

How to pop an Ollie

1) *Set your stance.* Stand on the board with the ball of your back foot hanging off the tail. The ball of your front foot should be in the middle of the deck, between the bolts.
2) *Crouch.* Keep your shoulders in line with your feet.
3) *Jump. Kick down* with your back foot so the board's tail hits the ground. The board should 'pop' off the ground.
4) *Bend your front knee* and *slide your front foot* towards the board's nose.

LOOK CLOSER

How did the Ollie get its name?
Alan Gelfand invented the Ollie in 1976. Gelfand's nickname was Ollie, so when he came up with the new trick, it was given the same nickname!

5) While still in the air, bring your back knee up to your chest. *Press down with your front foot.* Adjust the position of both feet so that the board levels out.
6) *Land both feet at the same time,* one above each truck. Let your knees bend when you hit the ground to absorb the impact.

Gravity: The attractive force exerted by any object with mass.

Ramps and Pipes

A skater launches into the sky. Then, still in midair, he or she spins around and drops back down on to the ramp. This classic vert trick uses simple laws of physics to reach whole new heights.

To get big air, you need to be moving at top speed.

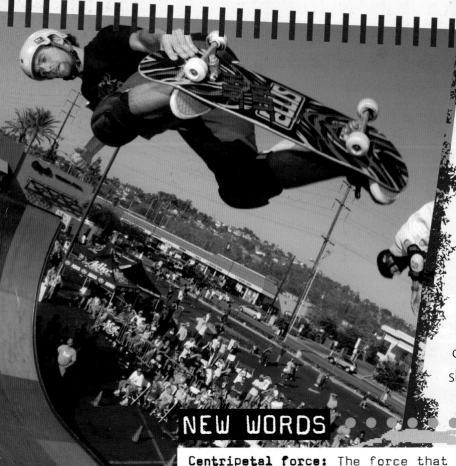

To move at speed, skaters crouch on the floor of the pipe and stand tall on the transition. This is called pumping. It works in the same way as pumping your legs on a swing makes you go higher and faster.

Skating force

Centripetal force keeps objects moving along a circular path. When you skate a half-pipe, centripetal

NEW WORDS

Centripetal force: The force that keeps objects moving in a circular path.

FACT!

▶▶▶▶▶▶▶▶

Skate to rotate

You need to apply a twisting force to start rotating. Skaters use their arms to create the **torque** for midair turns.

⬆ *Some skaters use empty pools as makeshift ramps.*

force acts on your body, keeping you in a crouch. To rise up, you need to work to overcome the force. Your extra effort produces more energy than you use, so you wind up not only beating the centripetal force, but boosting yourself up and over the lip.

LOOK CLOSER

Skating the ramp

Here's what you need to do to work the ramp:
· Drop in.
· On the floor, crouch.
· On the transition, stand up.
· Pull an Ollie at the lip and you will be airborne.
· Pull your legs up.
· Twist your upper body. Your legs and feet will turn in the opposite direction.
· Guide the board around with your front foot. Keep your legs tucked.
· As you descend, straighten your legs.
· Stay loose when you make contact. Let your knees absorb the shock.

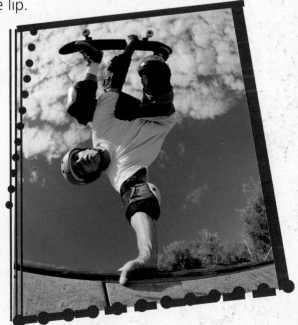

⬆ *Strength and balance are key to successful lip tricks.*

Torque: A twisting force.

Build Your Own Ramp

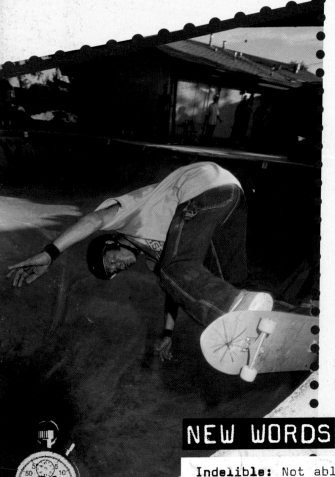

Tony Alva, one of the original Z-boys, skates in a pool.

To build your own ramp, all you need are simple materials and basic woodworking skills. Make sure an adult is available to supervise your work!

Z-boys

Back in the 70s, the Z-boys left an **indelible** mark on skateboarding. A surf shop in Venice, California, sponsored a local surfing team called the Zephyrs, or Z-boys for short. The Z-boys also skateboarded. Around that time, California was suffering from drought. A lot of people drained their swimming pools. The Z-boys would sneak into backyards and skate in the empty pools until the police showed up! Every day, the skaters would try something new. They ended up developing a new style of skateboarding. In 1975, at the *Del Mar Nationals*, the Zephyr team's thrilling moves caused a sensation. The Z-boys became stars. The team only lasted a few months before it was torn apart by fame and rivalries.

NEW WORDS

Indelible: Not able to be erased

24

Build your own ramp

1) Choose plans that you like and that will fit in your available space. You can find a lot of ideas on the Internet.

2) Cut all your pieces to size.

3) Build the framework, making sure all of the bracing is sturdy.

4) Soak the top sheets of plywood in cold water for about one hour. The water will soften the wood, making it easier to curve into shape.

5) Screw the plywood top sheets onto the framework.

6) Sand and paint the ramp to reduce friction and yield a smoother ride.

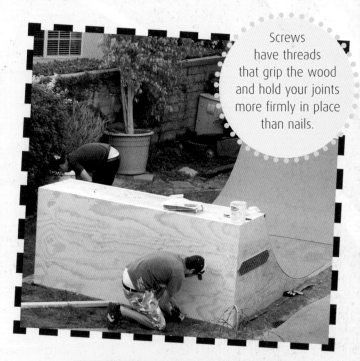

Screws have threads that grip the wood and hold your joints more firmly in place than nails.

What you need

Wood for the framework
Pen
Electric or handheld saw
Wood screws
Electric drill
Gaffer tape
Plywood sheets
Sandpaper
Paint

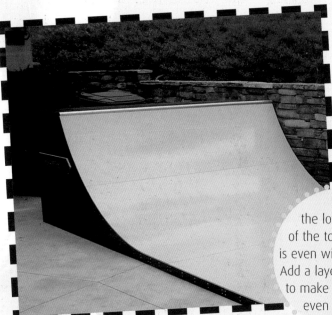

Sand the lowest edge of the top sheet so it is even with the ground. Add a layer of duct tape to make the transition even smoother.

Speed and Slalom

Street luge is an exciting alternative to conventional skating.

Got the need for speed? Downhill, slalom and other styles of speedboarding have been attracting fans since the earliest days of the sport.

Downhill skaters use extra-long rigid skateboards to **bomb** down hills at thrilling speeds. They wear **aerodynamic** helmets to reduce friction caused by wind resistance. Slalom skaters race through a track marked with small cones. They weave through the cones in the fastest possible time. The trick to good slalom skating is to pick the best 'line' through the course. In street luge and buttboarding, riders lie on their backs and hit speeds of up to 50 km/h (30 mph).

LOOK CLOSER

Safety gear

At high speeds, safety gear is essential. Racers suit up like motorcycle riders in full leather body 'armour', heavy gloves, protective footwear and DOT helmets.

NEW WORDS

Bomb: To go downhill as fast as you can.

Gravity racing

Skateboard racing is powered only by the force of gravity – no engines are allowed. An organisation called Gravity Sports International sponsors and oversees competition in all types of gravity-powered sports.

Pumping

A technique called pumping lets slalom skaters speed up with every turn they carve. To do so, skaters force their boards along an S-curved path by rocking their bodies and swinging their arms back and forth. Their motion generates so much energy that some skaters can even accelerate going up hills.

FACT!

▶ ▶ ▶ ▶ ▶ ▶ ▶ ▶

Dead Stop!

- Slalom and downhill skaters reach speeds of 60 km/h (40 mph).
- Top racers tape their shoelaces to increase their aerodynamics.
- Sliding – a form of stopping – has developed into a new type of downhill skateboarding.

Downhill skaters accelerate down a hill during a race in Aviemore in Scotland.

LOOK CLOSER

Body position

Downhill racers crouch to decrease wind resistance and pick up speed down the hill. To slow down, they 'air brake' by standing upright with arms outstretched.

Aerodynamic: Having a shape that improves the flow of air past it.

Future of Skateboarding

What might skateboarding look like in the future? Check out these possibilities, already in the works.

Michael J. Fox as Marty McFly on a hoverboard in the movie Back to the Future II *(1985).*

Will skateboarding, born in the laid-back world of surfing, always retain its freewheeling spirit? Maybe not. The skaters of the future will have to be ultra-fit athletes to keep up with the demands of their sport. They will have to train harder and smarter. Advances in sports medicine and technology will undoubtedly be used to improve skating technique, injury recovery and equipment design.

Hoverboards

The illusion of Michael J. Fox as Marty McFly skating on a **hoverboard** looks set to become a reality. To work, these flying decks need to be superlight. Look for high-tech components made of carbon nanotubes.

Ramping up

Imagine a half-pipe eight stories high. That's how big the megaramp is in the backyard of champion

NEW WORDS

Hoverboard: Skateboard-type vehicle that travels on a cushion of air.

Pro skater Danny Way launches off the DC Mega Ramp at Point X Camp in California.

Tomorrow's skaters will train hard to cope with the physical demands of their sport.

skater Bob Burnquist. As the ramps keep getting bigger, you can expect the vert tricks to get increasingly dangerous.

Skate simulation

Combine video games with the latest in **virtual reality** and what have you got? Simulated slides, flips and turns. That's extreme skateboarding without the risk.

Virtual reality: A computer-generated world in which people can interact with their environment.

Glossary

Aerodynamic: Having a shape that improves the flow of air past it.

Axle: A rod that attaches to wheels and allows them to spin.

Bomb: To go downhill as fast as you can.

Bushing: A hollow sleeve used to reduce friction or motion in mechanical parts.

Centre of gravity: The point in your body where your weight is centred.

Centripetal force: The force that keeps objects moving in a circular path.

Coordination: When the body and brain work together to balance and move.

Cruising: Using your board to move around.

Deck: The flat part of the skateboard on which the skater stands.

Dehydration: An unhealthy loss of water from the body.

Exoskeleton: An outer skeleton or shell, like the shell of an insect.

Friction: The force that opposes the movement of two surfaces that are touching one another.

Gender: Whether someone is male or female.

Gravity: The attractive force exerted by any object with mass.

Grind: To ride on a ledge or rail in such a way that only the trucks touch, making a grinding noise.

Half-cab: A ramp trick named for skater Steve Caballero.

Half-pipe: A U-shaped ramp used for tricks.

Hoverboard: Skateboard-type vehicle that travels on a cushion of air.

Immobilise: To prevent from moving.

Impact: When two objects hit each other, such as your feet and the ground.

Indelible: Not able to be erased.

Kicktail: The rise at the back of the deck.

Resilient: Being able to return to an original shape or position.

Sir Isaac Newton (1642–1727): English scientist who devised the three laws of motion.

Torque: A twisting force.

Urethane: A hard-wearing plastic that can be molded into different shapes.

Virtual reality: An artificial world in which people can interact with their environment.

Vulcanized: Soles with sulphur added to the rubber to make the shoes harder, stronger and more stretchy.

Find Out More

Books

Bowden, Rob. *Skateboarding (No Limits).* Franklin Watts, 2005.

Goodman, Polly. *Exercise and Your Body.* Wayland, 2007.

Horsley, Andy. *Skateboarding (To The Limit).* Wayland, 2008.

Powell, Ben. *Skateboarding (Extreme Sports).* Franklin Watts, 2003.

Stutt, Ryan. *Skateboarding: Landing the Basic Tricks.* A&C Black, 2009.

Websites

San Francisco's Exploratorium website is devoted to the science of skateboarding and includes video webcasts, activities and a glossary of unusual terms.

http://www.exploratorium.edu/skateboarding/

Find out how skaters utilise some basic laws of physics to perform amazing tricks such as the Ollie and frontside 180.

http://www.kidzworld.com/article/5207-the-science-of-skateboarding

The popular How Stuff Works website includes an article on skateboarding. Find out everything from the origins of the sport to step-by-step instructions on how to perform some of the basic tricks.

http://entertainment.howstuffworks.com/skateboarding.com

News, tips and advice from fellow skateboard enthusiasts in the UK.

http://www.sk8uk.co.uk/

Index